SECOND SKY

The Poiema Poetry Series

Poems are windows into worlds; windows into beauty, goodness, and truth; windows into understandings that won't twist themselves into tidy dogmatic statements; windows into experiences. We can do more than merely peer into such windows; with a little effort we can fling open the casements, and leap over the sills into the heart of these worlds. We are also led into familiar places of hurt, confusion, and disappointment, but we arrive in the poet's company. Poetry is a partnership between poet and reader, seeking together to gain something of value—to get at something important.

Ephesians 2:10 says, "We are God's workmanship . . ." *poiema* in Greek— the thing that has been made, the masterpiece, the poem. The Poiema Poetry Series presents the work of gifted poets who take Christian faith seriously, and demonstrate in whose image we have been made through their creativity and craftsmanship.

These poets are recent participants in the ancient tradition of David, Asaph, Isaiah, and John the Revelator. The thread can be followed through the centuries—through the diverse poetic visions of Dante, Bernard of Clairvaux, Donne, Herbert, Milton, Hopkins, Eliot, R. S. Thomas, and Denise Levertov—down to the poet whose work is in your hand. With the selection of this volume you are entering this enduring tradition, and as a reader contributing to it.

—D.S. Martin
Series Editor

COLLECTIONS IN THIS SERIES INCLUDE:

Six Sundays toward a Seventh by Sydney Lea
Epitaphs for the Journey by Paul Mariani
Within This Tree of Bones by Robert Siegel
Particular Scandals by Julie L. Moore
Gold by Barbara Crooker
A Word In My Mouth by Robert Cording
Say This Prayer into the Past by Paul Willis
Scape by Luci Shaw
Conspiracy of Light by D. S. Martin

Second Sky

Poems

TANIA RUNYAN

 CASCADE *Books* • Eugene, Oregon

SECOND SKY
Poems

The Poiema Poetry Series 10

Cascade Books
An Imprint of Wipf and Stock Publishers
199 W. 8th Ave., Suite 3
Eugene, OR 97401

www.wipfandstock.com

ISBN 13: 978-1-62564-288-2

Cataloging-in-Publication data:

Runyan, Tania.

    Second sky : poems / Tania Runyan.

    x + 74 p.; 23 cm.

    The Poiema Poetry Series 10

    ISBN 13: 978-1-62564-288-2

    1. 2. I. Title II. Series

PS3618.U5668 S43 2013

Manufactured in the USA.

The writing of *Second Sky* was supported in part by an award from the National Endowment for the Arts.

Eutychus Raised From the Dead
Acts 20:1–7

I, too, have slumped
at the sound of Paul's voice,
plummeted from the ledge,
the skeleton of my belief
disjointed and smashed.

But sometimes he stops
just long enough to find me
bleeding. Sometimes he takes
my face in his rough hands,
                    and I wake.

Contents

Contents

Acknowledgements

The Christian Century: Ananias Speaks to Saul (as Ananias of Damascus); Areopagus; Buried With Him In His Death; Count it All as Loss; The Ethiopian Eunuch; How Great a Struggle I Have For You; May the Word Run Swiftly, No One Can Boast; Not By Sight, Put on the New Self, We Cannot Take Anything Out of This World

Crannog: All Creation Groans

Cresset: The Prison Guard at Philippi Speaks (as The Prison Guard at Philippi); The Road to Damascus (as Damascus)

Harvard Divinity Bulletin: Groanings Too Deep for Words; Paul Speaks to Elymas About Blinding Him (as Paul's Blinding of Elymas)

Image: Before All Things; Onesimus Speaks (as Onesimus)

Literature and Belief: The Faith to be Made Well (as Your Faith Has Made You Well)

The Louisville Review: Newness of Life

The Other Journal: Perfected By the Flesh; Width, Length, Height, Depth; Visiting the Museum After a Charismatic Church Service (as Manifestation)

Rock & Sling: Lydia, Dealer in Purple Cloth; Not With Words of Eloquent Wisdom

Acknowledgements

Ruminate: How Great a Struggle I Have for You

Saint Katherine Review: Approach With Boldness (as Breaking the Surface), Artemis of Ephesus, Saul Complains About the Way

Sehnsucht: Who Will Deliver Me From This Body of Death?

I extend my deepest thanks to The National Endowment for the Arts, whose gift of a Literature Fellowship made the completion of this book possible.

Setting My Mind

Driving home from Pekin, IL

Salt spews from a cavalcade of trucks,
but still the icy shoulders of the road advance.
I maneuver my minivan over a licorice stick of asphalt.

My family laughs about the Abominable Snowman
stomping up I-55 and toppling
a truck-stop Dairy Queen.

I try to fight my imagining mind:
a bamboo foot-bridge sways over a river,
a quarter-inch slip and plunge into white.

They've taken the side of the storm,
this morning's Doppler watercolor
now a miracle birth in our headlights.

I pray that I can unclench and love,
find the mysteries of the Spirit
in swaths of black ice, the arms

of Christ in the muscled mounds of snow.
The exits count down toward home.
We're safe, I say, *we're safe, I'm safe.*

The kids trace their names in the foggy glass,
flakes like alyssum flowers
blurring their faces in the window.

Groanings Too Deep For Words

The morning I read about the newborn
found in the fast food dumpster,
heard the neighbor slam the door
on her *idiot whore* of a daughter,
and stepped on a Lego with my bare feet,
the magma of my own anger rising
with terrible speed, I grabbed the spade
from its winter storage and plunged
the cold steel into the earth.

Wars raged. My eyelid twitched.
But there was no prayer to save us,
just the lifting and turning of March's thaw,
my shovel crunching like a chant.
I wanted to curl into the clay, nest among
the locust nymphs lodged there like fetal hearts.
I lifted a clod throbbing with earthworms
and didn't wipe my hands. I kept them there,
wet and alive, squeezing through my fingers.

God's Folly

1 Cor 1:25

A dozen children pose on a hill of garbage in Indonesia,
gap-toothed little girls in sundresses linking arms in the front,
boys with hair in their eyes waving peace fingers in the back.

It's hard to accept their smiling in the sludge midway
through a twelve-hour shift picking for cans and cardboard.
We want the smudged faces, the flies swarming around crying mouths.

We want to save them from the feces and gristle steaming
in the sun, the syringes and carcasses under their bare feet.
Oh, to swoop them from the bulldozers and wrap

their rat bites and rashes, to give them bowls of spaghetti
and tuck them in lavender sheets! But for now, this boy will have
none of it. A few pieces of scrap metal in his burlap sack,

he takes a moment to celebrate, kicking a rotten grapefruit
through two table legs. *Goooal!* His brother tags him
with blackened fingers, and they run off, their tattered shirts

flying like kite tails. Behind a truck, a little girl bounces as she pokes
through a fresh heap with a stick. She unearthed the arm of a doll
this morning—the best find in four years of scavenging.

She keeps it in her pocket and all afternoon strokes its melted
plastic fingers. As the sun goes down, she takes it out
and rests it in the crook of her arm, imagines it whole.

Newness of Life

South African man wakes after 21 hours in morgue fridge

What cold salvation,
dragging fingernails
through the frost

of a half-dream
then waking
to a plastic cocoon.

The louder you scream
from your aluminum drawer
the more they believe

you're a ghost come
to haul them inside.
I feel your shivering

in my own bones,
stumble with you
into the vicious light.

Some burst alive
on the pyres of the Spirit.
Some blink open

slowly, alone, packed in ice:
How did I get here?
I never knew I was dead.

No One Can Boast

Eph 2:9

On the toll way just south of Kenosha
spring sets the boarded-up porn store ablaze,
topaz dousing the peeling paint,
the harp-notes of ice on the gutters.
On the embankment home geese gather
in the mud-slush. Tractors lift their beams
to the rising temple of a new overpass.

I outlasted winter, four months rumpled
under snow. On Christmas we woke
to a broken furnace, the baby's fingers
carrot-stick cold. One night I skidded
off the patio steps. Most mornings I stared
out the window, wondering how far
I'd driven my life in the ground,
asking the darkness how much longer.

I kill the radio. Just the hum of the motor,
the pitted road, my slow, steady breath
like the syllables *Yah, weh.* I didn't work
at this joy. It just appeared in the splash
and shine of I-94, as suddenly as these Frisbees
and sand buckets in the roadside yards
laid bare by the shrinking snow.

Before the world was made.
Your nebula of breath.
Yin-yangs of tadpole eggs
frozen inside a star.

I was just a dream, a single
neuron firing. But there was
something I wanted to say
to you, something like

I won't be saved,
my invisible fists rising.
The world did not deserve
my mercy, other that it was.

You knew then
that I would return, standing here
at the kitchen sink:
I can't scrub a pan without you.

Let there be light, you said,
and I hid my face.
I can see you,
and you are good.

Awake, O Sleeper

Eph 5:24

And rise up—
Your son is calling you.

Mama!—A helicopter zips
high above the backyard maples—*Mama!*

He points to the sky and tugs.
You don't look up. You falsetto

a *Yay* and keep on
deadheading the pansies.

He is two, with small wants
and small things to say.

Your life looms with all you must save.
He walks off to follow the sky alone.

When you were small,
growing up by the freeway,

you waited for the rush hour
choppers to make their

traffic rounds: nose-heavy,
transparent dragonflies

with headphoned men
leaning into the controls.

You waved at them,
first a hand, then both arms flailing.

You spun on roller skates,
twirled a rainbow windsock

until finally one day
a hand shot up.

This was your closest thing
to answered prayer.

And with the rhythm of the chop
inside you—even now you feel it—

you walk across the yard
to grab his hand.

Approach with Boldness *Eph 3:12*

Yellowstone National Park

We creak on boardwalks above geothermal pools—
Black Opal, Morning Glory, Emerald Spring.
Clear and bright as cups of Easter dye,
they sputter and hiss to remind us that we stand
atop a caldera heaving molten rock.

Each path begins with the illustrated warning:
a boy in a baseball cap breaks through the surface,
parboiling his feet. I hear the story about the 9-year-old
who lost himself in the steam and plunged into Crested Pool.
They recovered just eight pounds of his body.

Or the man who swan-dived into Celestine Pool
after a yelping dog, emerging with blanched irises.
That was dumb, he mumbled for his last words,
skin peeling in sheets. Thousands of years ago
the first hunter to wander into this basin

must have thought he discovered a second sky
breaking through the ground, a miracle of sorts,
if he knew about those, radiating in the snow.
He laughed, bent his face over the rising steam,
and thought nothing of reaching in.

Whatever is Lovely

Phil 4:8

My son climbs a pile of wobbling logs
   strung with spider webs,
the last week of summer
   flickering in his hair.
He lifts his arms—balance and praise—
   carpenter bees rolling out
of the loosened bark.

A half-inch of flip-flop
   holds him by the heels—
I must allow him this—
   the maple fell two winters ago
in heavy snow, and now
   he can ascend the pyramid
on his own, write his name in the air.

Pass, lovely moment,
   and keep his neck intact.
For look: he's already slipping
   and scraping all the way down.
Don't look at me! he shouts,
   then feels the blood on his chin.
Hey! Now I've got a goatee!

Not With Words of Eloquent Wisdom   *1 Cor 1:17*

Lest the cross be emptied of its power.
So let's shoot straight about that one cedar seed
that slipped from a cone of thorns
and forced its sapling among a hundred others,
ignorant of its future on buildings and altars
or dangling from women's ears.
It stood by the daily torture of falcons
plunging for rabbits and voles, of blood
blackening the needles where the deer stared blank
at her stillborn fawn. And when the ax swung
in the hands of the exhausted solider
who knew nothing of prophecy and everything
of rattling toward death, it was just another quake,
another storm ripping its branches to the ground,
another day riding on the shoulders of the accused.

He has the face of an angel:
soft, androgynous, fire in his hair.
Petals of blood seep through his mantle
as his arm swings for balance.

The stones continue to weave their flight.
A conglomerate rock, brown flex
of muscle, takes aim at his bowing head.

Once two continents collided,
and a river squeezed through a mountain.
Quartz and calcite fused and spun
a new earth on the bottom of the stream.

The stone has settled in the hands
of a laundress, in the shepherd's fire,
and, briefly, in the sky when a boy
hurled it into a torrent of stars.

Now the stone glances off Stephen's face.
Blood and sediment cling to his hair.
Quartz glistens, bones crack,
the arm bends under his fall.
Dust to dust to dust.

The Prince of the Power of the Air Eph 2:2

You brought me to this kingdom of fluorocarbons,
where kites get tangled in power lines
and fuselages break apart over the sea.

You gave me to the body's longings—
I tracked the clouds from my bed for hours
as the baby cried in another room

and the neighbor went on dying.
The radio waves seized me—
I sang along to the power of my senses

and the weakness of faith, followed satellites
to a wonderland of plastic,
breathed the acid rain, the valley's smog.

Then I came loose and fell through
the torrents of wings and wind.
There was the ground, the wet stones,

the twisted roots of the great oak
waiting.

Saul Complains About the Way

Acts 9:1

As if You hadn't dropped manna
into their crying mouths, as if Your voice
hadn't flared from the brambles, they proclaim
a new spirit in their bodies, that dove
that swooped down on the blasphemer
now beating inside them with frenzied wings.

They bow before a decomposing criminal
who hung on a tree like a curse,
who spoke with women spilling sex from their tunics,
and groped the sores of lepers on Your day.
What's next: eating hawks and swine, dressing children
in mildew, lying with menstruating wives?

As I bind their wrists, they pray for me—
a Hebrew of Hebrews needing prayer!
Even as the ropes cut in, they pour out
their hymns, giving me cheek after cheek after cheek
as I gouge them out at the root, these wild shoots
that sprout in our vineyard, tangling You up.

The Road to Damascus

1.
Mine is not a sin-tacular story
of stumbling up the steps to the heroin clinic,
prostituting my way through prom night
or mangling my children in the slot machine—
no crazy here—

just a silent road to Damascus,
a pin-hole light through a curtain,
a glaucomatous cloud
that no Ananias would heal.
My persecution was too weary
for fame, a low-grade virus burying Christ
under the sweaty blankets of winter.

2.
When you slog a muddy path
through the woods and denounce the rain,
you blaspheme him. When the blackbird
shrills outside your window at five a.m.
and you count each shrill as a strike
against you, you drag him to jail.
When you curse the train-track suicide
for making you late, you swing the scourge
of stones above your head.

3.
All the while he had me figured out—
infuriating now to think of it— how he followed
my bike down the riverbed to the beach,
knowing my arms would blister
as I lay there seeking faith
in my body; how he watched me
count free throws, eight out of ten times

the ball banking off the edge or swirling from the rim
like a dog circling his sick bed. I wasted hours
on the blacktop with no poetry or prayer.
He knew I would come.
He knew if I stood long enough
in the chain-link echoes of miss and miss,
I would let the ball roll into the roses to stay.

4.

Some say Saul had a grand mal seizure
in the middle of the road—falling sickness,
they called it then—the temporal lobes tenderized
to the flashing lights and sounds of God,
then the transient blindness. There you have it:
a world institution born of a disorder in the brain.
It makes sense now, my pregnancies
driving me to pray over the toilet bowl,
night sweats stirring up heavenly visions,
the swollen nodule bringing me to weep for mercy.
It was in the imagination of my body all along,
this diagnosis of faith, the spirit's feverish work.

5.

In sixth grade I started to fear the end of things.
The planets will align, the news said.
The sun's imbalance will churn the atmosphere,
set the Earth off-kilter and shift the plates
like boards in a speeding hatchback.
So instead of conjugating Spanish verbs
I stared at the deceitful sky. Unfair
that my braces had yet to shift my woodchuck
bite, that my violining languished in a first-position
Ode to Joy. No boobs. No boys.
No high school science labs with lime-green tubes
or a college freezer full of Klondike bars.
I had no choice but to lay it down.
My voice, my flash of light
the silver marble of Jupiter smoldering
before dawn, rolling closer to my window.

6.
I have sinned, I said.
I want eternal life, I said.
That was the moment.
I wanted nothing but God.
I wanted a cheeseburger.
I wanted nothing at all.
Finally, I wanted it settled.
I folded my hands and spoke
to the carpet. I folded my hands
and spoke to the Lord.
I woke up and felt no different.
I woke up and my life
came to an end.

7.
Saul lay blind for a few days.
Then the scales fell from his eyes
and he started proclaiming His name.

I still have the scales, God,
my eyes a salmon's skin:
green and lavender sunrise
on a thousand mottled hilltops.
The salmon fling themselves
upstream, shaking their bodies
free of rainbow specks,
losing the promise
in the flood. I'm trying to see,
God, trying to break through
this shine of darkness.
Each day another scale falls,
and another covers my eye.

8.
If only it could be as easy as Paul,
to curse one day and bless

the next, repent and change direction
for good. Not this cycling of faith:
a little light in the morning, lifting a hand
in prayer, then dozing to the bore
of the spirit. My body doesn't cling
to Philippian prison bars
or risk martyrdom
but saunters through the valley
of the shadow of ease. God saved
the Corinthians from their temple orgies,
rescued serial killers from their incinerated
hearts. Can he save me again,
a woman too laggard to lose any hope,
too blind to collapse in a flash of light?

The Day is at Hand

Shaving Day at the Monastery, *Eduard Gruntzer (1887)*
Milwaukee Art Museum

They enter the room with bowed heads,
ready to consecrate their faces to God

and remove the shadows that draw
over their chins like the temple veil.

But as soon as the barber slathers
the first stoic jawbone, the abbott

crumples into laughter, and then they all
fall under the spell of those thick hands

spreading a Sistene ceiling of clouds,
the razor's silvery pulse.

They look in the mirror with no worry
of vanity, even the nick at the throat

a tiny stigmata of joy. And oh,
that first hour when their hoods slip

across their skin like the breezes
on their boyhood faces

when they hiked the hillsides
and received their callings, or, perhaps,
    the wind.

Perfected By the Flesh

Bronze Woman IV, *Thomas Schutte*
Minneapolis Sculpture Garden

She, too, can no longer hold
her flesh together,
the folds and heft of the commandments
she has carried for so long
finally collapsing on themselves.
She lies on her wooden slab
like Isaac on the altar.
I run my hands
over the splayed bronze
of her shoulder and breast,
exhale my failures
to keep anything holy.
Beyond us the bridges and towers
of the cold city extend
into their lonely, lawful places.
Our tarnished lips mouth *Abba, Father*,
gaping in the frost.

Ananias Speaks to Saul   *Acts 9:17 –18*

Saul, you thug who once dragged
believers through the streets,

flinging them from their beds so hard
their arms popped from their sockets,

how like a dying child you look,
your stomach caved in from fasting,

lips blistered with fevered prayer.
You reach into the darkness, trembling

from the exhaustion of reliving
the scene: *The light shot out of the sky—*

no, it flared from the stones—no,
Jesus, you were on fire—

God spoke to me, too. Which is why
I stand at your bedside now and beseech

the Spirit to enter. He loves to appear
in the lonely, dank rooms of the faithful:

Daniel, Mary, Abraham, all sweating out
their dreams of God. You will learn

how hard belief can be. You will sing
while guards whip you to the bone,

touch an enemy's shoulder with grace
while the avenging knife burns at your hip.

One day you will wish for your sick bed again,
this woolen blanket of blindness.

But I do as I am told. I lay my fingertips
on your lids, and your eyes rumble

like stones rolling from the grave. Your lids
creak open, and the light burns through.

This healing is not easy. Something silver
falls from your eyes. Brother, something

like the scales of a struggling fish
scatter at my feet.

Every Knee Shall Bow

Phil 2:10

Someone spends her whole life
ducking the bloody feet of the crucifix

or occasionally patting His shiny hair:
Nice Jesus. You do magic with fish.
Now move your pansy ass.

And now she's knocked behind the kneecaps
and pitched to the street,
trading her skin for stones.

This is belief? Blubbering *Christ*
because he snuck up on you,
shadowed you with stealth-bomber wings?

I'll take it, he says, *your eleventh-hour*
whimpering, knees skinned from skating
too fast. Anything will make

this human-form thing worth it.
Any noise you make to me joyful.

Lydia, Dealer in Purple Cloth Acts 16:14

She did well. Twelve thousand mollusks
had to be dredged from the sea
and crushed to dye one royal hem.

After baptism, she thought of the shells.
She felt the water puddle in the swirl
of her ear, a streamlet run down her spine.

Next market day she watched
the silks and linens deepen in the sun
and lowered her lips to the folds.

Put on the New Self

Col 3:10

Twenty-five years after Praying the Prayer,
when my new life was supposed to snap in place
like elastic, the smell of crisp, store-rack cotton
propelling me to run with endurance
toward a finish line I could not see,

I lie on the couch with a sour-smelling terrier
curled in the crook of my leg. Today
I will bathe him, punch through three K-cups,
run a trumpet book to the grammar school.
No martyrdom here, no preaching in the streets,
though tomorrow I might plant another bag of daffodils
so in April I can kneel in the gold
and thank All Things New once more.

But now I turn my eyes to things above
in the window, squirrels gibbering in the canopy
of my backyard maple. I doze and wake
to their claws skittering down the trunk,
mentally etch the face of Christ in the bark.

He doesn't need me. He wants me.
Neither Jew nor Greek, male nor female, tired
nor on fire. I will slip into newness again,
fluff the shaking, sodden dog in His name
as He drapes me with his soft and silent weaving.

Who Will Deliver Me From This Body of Death? *Rom. 7:24*

Beast XVI, bronze, 1959, Lynn Chadwick
Frederik Meijer Gardens and Sculpture Park, Grand Rapids, MI

Not a Michelangelo after God's own heart
but a pancaked boar with a dent eye
and stump snout, triangles piled on chopstick legs.

Still, beast, you are lovely in your darkness.
I want to lay my head
on the cool edges of your body, that waterfall

of Lazurus' fingers. If I let you loose
they'd shoot a dart in your rump
before you could lumber through the park
head-butting children and snapping the tendrils
of Chihuly glass. But you wouldn't do that.

You would sink into a secluded pond
and snuffle the lilies and cattails,
then silently watch the sky in the water
until curtains of emerald algae
rippled from your skeletal back.

Paul Proclaims in the Synagogue

Acts 9:20–22

With my eyes come back to me
all of Damascus is dreamy and lit

as if seen through a locust wing
held to the sun.

The prayer fringe brushes my legs
like rain, and I can breathe

now, breathe as I run to the synagogue
where the rabbis crush in,

shouting for one of my prison grabs.
How easy it had always been

to make them love me:
wrench, rope, and scourge.

Wash out the Way's *blasphemy*
with their own blood.

But now the believers' faces
spread over these columns

like morning in the trees
and *Christ is Messiah*

leaps from my stomach,
runs to the edge of my mouth

like Legion's pigs.
The fierce bodies of these words

bump against each other
in a grunting blur

like my bunching tongue and lips
till the hand of the Spirit

pushes them off. Like I, too,
am falling, flying past

the daggers of crags
on the way down,

the men looking over the ledge
with hands in the air,

spitting and shouting,
and the brilliant churning sea beneath.

The Prison Guard at Philippi Speaks   *Acts 16:25 –28*

At night they should become less
than the animals they are, like the mildew lining
these piss-splashed walls.
They should lay down their matted heads,
be still and know the piled dead
decomposing in the corner.

To shift is to scrape the shackles
that wake your brethren to their lust
for bread. To struggle is to rust the metal
with your sweat. No telling how deep the cuts
when the blood runs in the darkness, when your wounds
stick to your partners' in chains.

And what foolishness to give breath to singing
when the air is scarce, to shout to a god
as your lungs fill with phlegm! As if
he would peer into the midnight of thieves,
reach down into these huddled bodies
swarming with maggots and lice.

It's enough to make the earth break open,
the walls collapse, and oh—
the inmates stepping over the twisted bars
with shackles hanging!—
It's enough
to make anyone want to die.

Count it All as Loss

Phil 3:7

All of it: children whistling ryegrass,
my husband rubbing my back

in his sleep. Consider rubbish the sun
climbing the eye of Delicate Arch,

the scent of popped-open coffee.
Leave it behind, pleads the scourge-

scarred Paul. Lay it down and rise.
But even loss is hard to count as loss.

This morning frost has leathered
the nasturtium, but I cannot endure

ripping the haloes of leaves from their pot.
The astilbe, once a lavender mist

in my window, burns toward winter,
seed heads trembling like the hands

of an old charismatic. Maybe in heaven
I will remember the March I buried

those bare roots around the base of the oak
and brooded about some sin or another

holding me fast in the mud, spring
the only unseen I could bear to believe.

Hard to find it, yes, among all the CNN corpses,
a gospel spreading anywhere but through the sewage drains.

But most fruit is invisible as the clouds of mushroom spores
we part with our hiking boots. They cling to rocks and logs

as their God spreads for an acre underground: She gets out of bed.
He puts down the syringe. Father revs his bike to come home for good.

The teenager pulls on her checkered socks, thinking she'd rather die
than walk those halls again, thinking about that death.

On TV she hears about a near-miss asteroid. Turn it off, her mom says.
But no—this was as close as God got to pitching fire through the sky.

Never mind the thousand Hiroshimas if it hit. *If I can become vapor,*
I am the matter that is conserved. I am before all things

like the angels in paintings whose faces blend into the sky.
She glides through the doors of her school. The kids keep looking

through her. O fragile invisible power! There is so much to do now,
the forgiving, the hand on the passing shoulder.

She reads the news. She traces the bodies on her laptop screen,
bows her head, and dares.

I Can Do All Things

Phil 4:13

Even stand in line for my first roller coaster
	at the age of forty-one—
stomach already lurching—
	but consider staying upright
sipping an eight-dollar soda
	the way of fools.

	Omniscience, yes. Cries rise
from the cancer clinics
	and droned-out fields.
I whisper *Jesus* as the car rickets
	to the top, *Save me*
as the first plunge swoops me into a loop,

	then another, asphalt flashing.
This matters: the right hand of God
	pressing against my shoulder harness
as I corkscrew through the sky
	and scream, his good
and faithful fool.

Paul Speaks After Blinding Elymas *Acts 13:8 –11*

Sometimes you must do out of love
what devastate the senses.

This wasn't easy, Elymas. I know
blindness, how suddenly

the specks in stones you can't see
become worth dying for.

From the way you grope this cloud of mist
I know you're trying to imagine

the colors of the stars right now,
the blue-white shine that once

ignited your hands with power.
But you can conjure only

the upturned bellies of poisoned frogs,
your mother's dying lips.

Don't you know how small
this life is? Even the stars

are just the sweat Christ shakes
from his brow. When you make crooked

the path to eternity, you send your brother
to oblivion, to the buried speck

in the midnight desert stone. This time,
no magic will save you. You

will have to find your life in the dark.
You will have to be led by the hand.

The Greatest of These   *1 Cor 13*

Embraces the woman whose child screams
on the floor of the cereal aisle.
Enters the friend's new mansion,
lifts eyes to the skylights, gives thanks.
Yields the last word on the Facebook fight.
Looks the frowning barista in the eye.
Takes a breath and thanks God
there is even a zipper to get stuck.
Sends a gift to the wall-punching uncle.
Glances away from the handcuffed boys
on the side of the road and prays.
Smiles and listens to the grandmother complain
about her knees, rubs the knees,
ladles another bowl of soup.
Believes there is a reason that slumped man
in the alley was born. Trusts he'll believe it.
Endures the quiet, thankless song of work.
Echoes long after the cymbals have died.

The Faith to Be Made Well

Acts 14:8–10

As I pray for my canker sore to disappear
I slide my tongue over the white groove
in my lip, knowing full well it will stay a few more days.

So I pray again, willing some holy
invasion of my flesh, like my friend who limped
to the altar and felt a thousand warm needles

stitching his herniated discs. *Believe,*
and you will be healed. I clamp my eyes tighter.
The sore sticks in my teeth like a seed.

I trust the clear scans of stage IV cancer patients,
testimonies of sunlight breaking through
cloudy eyes, cell-phone videos of straightened spines.

But God and I both know it doesn't happen
to people like me, people who make a home
of their tiny, stinging wounds,

who walk into a church and expect nothing
but dusty plastic lilies, fliers curling
on bulletin boards, the coffee pot's gurgle and hiss.

Cadillac Ranch

Gal 6:9

Amarillo, TX

No billboards or exit signs:
just ten junk Cadillacs
sunk nose-first in a field.

Every year we pull to the frontage
and slog through the chain gate
past hundreds of spent spray cans

and their flung-petal lids.
Wind whisks the cow piles
as roadtripping teens climb

through glassless windows
and a Babel of tourists
shout over their aerosol maracas.

We videotape our kids squinting
in the gnatted heat
and spraying their names

thickly over the others,
their letters red caterpillars
in the wheel wells.

They pose on undercarriages
blazing with peace signs,
7/2/12, and primitive genitalia,

Travis ♥'s Linda new enough
to bleed neon pink on their shirts.
Desperate blue *ADAMs*

36

splatter every tailfin, but within
a few hours all our signatures
will be covered again.

Like last year, I spray *Tania*
across an axle in lime green,
never tired of the amorphous

moss of it, for it matters, somehow,
my part in this wreck,
my name hidden under a thousand coats.

All Creation Groans

Not just people, but balled-up honeybees.
Polar bears clawing for crumbling floes.
The wind mourns as it strips the soil
from its own beloved hillside.
Fault lines pitch trees and stones
with the lurching sobs of the grieved.

It's hard to imagine what star, what sequoia
needs to await a blessed day of peace.
But even they must feel the gravitational pull
of dead leaves and beetle legs washing down
with the rain water, the vanishing bromeliads
holding out their cups.

Not By Sight

2 Cor 5:7

Railway therapy, Indonesia

*"As many as several dozen people per day intentionally try to electrocute them-
selves along the rails. . .because they believe it can cure all kinds of diseases. . ."*
–WALL STREET JOURNAL, AUGUST 6, 2011

The Jakartans offer themselves fully to the tracks,
a row of living crucifixes stretched across the rails.

They spread their arms along one side, sling their necks
back over the steel, and tilt their faces to the sky.

On the other track they prop their ankles, bare feet
pulsating to the low voltage of faraway trains.

They believe the charges emit sparks of insulin, release
the blue current of sleep, liquefy arthritic hands.

And when freight trains thunder by on parallel tracks,
wheels just feet from their trembling chests, they press

even further into the steaming metal, believing in a healing
no doctor has proved, no faithful like me has prayed for.

Coptic Church bombing, Alexandria, Egypt, 1/1/2011

All day they pray before the blood-splashed banner of Christ.
He spreads his robed arms into the browning clouds.
A young man leans into Jesus, tucking his head
beneath his chin. A woman presses her fingertips to his hair.

What is real are the rabbits' feet of winter buds
on the magnolia out front, the boards and plastic buckets
accumulating in the neighbor's yard. How great the struggle,
to unfold my arms and work my hands through

these frosted windows, to lay my fingers over that woman's
and feel the pulse of her grief. But I hold on. I want to slouch
back in my chair but hold until my hands sweat, until she sweats
into the bloody hair of Christ. How great the struggle

to stay here while the phone rings, to shove through God's
great shadow of *why*. We lean into the stain.
We feel the blood still pounding as it did through the man
who just hours ago lay himself open to prayer.

Paul Considers the Viper

Acts 28: 2–6

He did not deflect stones from my head,
stiffen my blood for two hundred lashes,

and sweep me to shore on a splintered plank
to let me die from two-inch fangs.

So I fling the snake into the fire,
where the body lurches and smolders to char.

Time to pray over the sick, of course, but the islanders
dare not approach. They stare at my hand,

the only sound cracking kindling and waves.
A trembling woman drops to the sand.

Christ, for a moment your face
has fallen below the horizon,

leaving me with a cooling faith,
a litany of visions and coincidences.

And these punctures I should have forgotten by now
rise toward me like your eyes on the cross

slowly disappearing in the weeping blood,
entreating, *why have you forsaken me?*

To Die is Gain

Phil 1:21

For Melissa, after the diagnosis

Even when she found herself
curled up on the deck of a ship

when the ocean began to bare its teeth,
she breathed deeply,

turned on her side, and watched him
sleep. His mouth hung open, arm coiled

over his head like the tail of a sated cat.
The Son of Man's cheek sank

into the valleys of his robe.
The rain began to hammer the deck—

and still she watched him—
even as it suddenly ripped sideways

through the sails. Water washed over
his calloused toes like a river

over stones. This is when
she saw the wall of water heaving

toward them, a flash of driftwood,
fish, and knotted kelp

towering over the gunwales. *Wake up!*
she screamed—she couldn't help it now—

Jesus, move! He opened one
drowsy eye, rolled it to her stricken face,

and locked it there. *I mean, let it come,*
she yawned. *Lord, Let it come.*

Or maybe not.

Do Not Be Anxious About Anything

Except for the moment when the landing gear
lifts from the pavement, the overhead compartments
cracking their knuckles. Then the First Great Turn
of the wing, which always threatens to bank too far
to the left. (112 degrees in the Chicago crash—
did they feel themselves invert?)

The problem is making someone's story your own.
Don't you realize that *is your suffering?*

I want to know if they died from impact or flames.

You're safer in a 747 than your shower.

The aerophobia forum pulsates today:
Canceling Reno!
Faulty flaps . . .
Singapore turbulence?
Freaking out!

These are my people: the ones who run to the bathroom
(again) before boarding, visualizing their flight numbers
in the headlines. They feel the long tunnel of the jet bridge
close on them—if they make it that far—
and slap the fuselage for good luck.
They search the cockpit for bloodshot eyes,
keep the plane aloft by counting, look for terror
in the attendants' faces with every bounce of air.

In 1986, a Piper clipped the tail of a DC-9.
The jet plunged, just miles from my home,
limbs and metal burning on the lawns.

You'd have to fly daily for 123,000 years
before your plane would go down.

But what if it did? What would I do
during that ten-second dive?
Yell, Here I come, God! *and open your arms.*
It's a good way to go. Better than cancer.
And besides, they always say you die before you hit.

Paul Insists He is Not a God

Acts 14:12

Just a man like you.
I've sat with you on your stone latrines
and scraped the dust from my ears.

So why these oxen lined up in offering,
the pungent garlands of lilies and herbs?
Bow to the one who made these,

who polished the shining fur as you slept
and dropped the pollen
from his fingertips. I do nothing

but let the spirit lift my hands to heal.
Blasphemers! Why raise the knife
of sacrifice? Haven't you seen me walk

my old, bowed legs to the hillsides
and pray to my holy invisibility?
I know your gods. Do you think

I haven't dreamt how divine life
would be as muscled Hermes,
listened to without the threat of stones?

To pull my winged cap over glistening curls,
tuck a staff under one arm and a soul under the other
and sail into that evil, easy underworld.

Man is Without Excuse

Perhaps you could say that in Rome, Paul,
where the olive trees of the Seven Hills

string their pearls of rain against the sky.
And yes, as I hike Glacier Park

with a well-stocked pack, I can welcome
God's ambassadors of fireweed and paintbrush,

the psalmic rhythm of lake hitting shore.
But as the refugee trudges

from Mogadishu to Dabaab, is she to catch
a glimpse of antelope bone in the thicket

and intuit the sufferings of the Son of Man?
She wears her own nails and crown.

An Eden of lizards surges at her heels,
but she wonders at nothing

but the sore-studded daughter she left to die
on the road, and now, the baby

strapped to her back: six pounds
at one year old. He no longer cries

but flutters small breaths on her neck
like the golden wings of moths

she counts with worshipful attention.

Paul Discusses His Healings at Ephesus   *Acts 19:11–12*

The dove that descended on Christ
and now makes his nest in my body

strains his wings against the walls
of my chest. I coax him out

of my fingertips—flight of heaven,
come—until he blazes through

with my skin on his claws.
People thrust fabric before me,

and when the Spirit sweeps down
I feel myself enter the weave:

the handkerchief a woman will wrap
around her husband's palsied hand,

the blanket the mother will press
to her baby's violet lips. A child falls

at my feet with his mother's apron.
She is trying to get the baby out

but only blood is coming.
I hold this cloth to my face and weep

into the birth fluid and blood,
the smoke from last night's meal.

As night falls, I feel it is I in their home—
not the apron, but my own hands draped

over the whimpering pulse in her wrists
as the baby screams in the corner for milk

and the father splits me with his stares,
wondering, Spirit, if we will come through.

Thorn

2 Cor 12:7

Vocal paralysis

One cord lies like a dead rubber band
while the other vibrates wildly for its partner,
slamming against the air. When I try to speak
my voice escapes in a quick deflation of vowels.

Paul asked three times for his thorn to be removed
then shrugged himself into faith. I walk in a state
of silent beseeching, fixated on the woman
who expends volcanic energy to laugh at nothing

and the man who yells, *Get your stupid ass
in the car*—as if it were so cheap and simple
to speak, to grip and funnel the air
through the folded membranes in the throat.

My daughter comes home and flings her coat
on the floor, galloping upstairs before catching
my look. I can only chase after her flouncing ponytail,
dumb and desperate and powerfully weak.

We Cannot Take Anything Out of This World   *1 Tim 6:7*

One of the few ways I can speak to you
is sliding nylon hairs over wound aluminum,

praying low arpeggios under the choir's hymn,
or reeling in the kitchen as the soup overflows.

Today I lamented by the window as autumn's
gray mushrooms beaded the foot of the maple tree.

Triple-stopped strings, slightly flattened,
my only real cry. You seemed to build heaven

for the air-spun singer who can bundle all the cords
of her body in a breath. But I need the language

of arm and bow, callous and vibrato, clouds
of rosin rising. Oh, let me keep it, Lord,

even when I rise from the grave,
this quavering voice, this scuffed hourglass of wood.

Buried With Him In His Death

We fought for one more sputter
of the old life. Even though a breeze passing
over your sieve of skin could send you
screaming, you muscled up your diaphragm
to whisk more air into the fire.

I held my own terrors to my chest:
failures and brush-offs, cancers and crashes,
all the anxieties I had grown to love
heaving and cracking like your ribcage
until we both gave out.

Then there was the mess of prying us loose:
wailing women and splintered lumber,
flesh stubbornly sticking to the nails.
But what swift hands, that Joseph of Arimathea,
what purposeful footsteps crunching the ground!

He wrapped us in linen and spices.
Only the hapless world could think of packing
fifty pounds of aloe around a dead man's wounds.
But we drank it in like deserts
until finally even the lizards scurried home.

I lay in the cave and wanted to touch you,
but my hands were no longer mine.
They closed in on themselves like daylilies.
The stone rumbled over the window of light,
and then our difficult rising began.

All We Ask Or Imagine

Eph 3:20

Lake Villa Township Park

By the park entrance, where the Saturn smacked the Harley,
our church picnic forms a fence of prayer
(or a few *Heavenly Father*'s for a glimpse of gore).

Getcher hands off me! the biker shouts at the EMTs. He staggers,
a curtain of blood in his face. Someone spins the kids
on the giant merry-go-round to blur the scene.

The hitters stand by their torn-off bumper
like losers at a dance. The floppy-haired teen clings
to his Gatorade, imprinting for life his father's failure to yield.

Let me go, you mothers! the victim screams as they angle
the stretcher into the ambulance. Black jeans,
black boots thrashing. So little he asked of his day

when he zipped them up at dawn, so narrow his imagination
when he kicked the stand and revved up to our town
for another Sunday of beer and brats. Later that night

I search the news and find that *Unnamed, 54*, is 90 miles
from home, hospitalized with extensive head injuries.
Heal him, Jesus, we had prayed out there. *Show up in this.*

So I have to believe that something good can come
from relearning your head. Maybe the ringing
in his ears will tune him to the heavens. Maybe forgetting

everything about his wife but the way she looked
washing her bike in a bikini in '82 will awaken
him to the newfound softness in her thighs.

He will no longer concentrate on many tasks at once.
The morning coffee and paper on his porch
will become a mesmerizing swirl of cream in his cup,

the swoop and trill of red-wings. He will learn to write his name
with slow, careful curlicues and lines: the word of the Lord.
He will stare in the mirror for hours: His image.

How Beautiful the Feet

Rom 10:15

San Bernardino, CA

Seventeen with a colicky baby slung over her arm—
the baby who slips off the nipple screaming,
shaking pink fists—
she paces the crushed river rocks
where her father had ripped out the lawn,
breasts heavy with failure.

She knows there are mountains
ten miles to the east, peaks submerged
in the smog. If she could just get past these ragged palms
with their graffitied trunks, without a car overheating
and a baby strapped in the back, she could breathe
blue, listen to the flickers drumming the sugar pines,
water rushing over her toe rings.

Even if someone in the forest loved her
she could stand another day
by imagining his imagining her
as he hiked through the pinions.
He could come down carrying the scent of needles,
even run to her like she runs to the baby
all night—imagine, being run for!—

his sandals descending the spiraling roads,
kicking up dirt and lizards by the freight tracks
in the foothills, pounding past fast food wrappers
caught in barbed-wire fences.
How beautiful those feet would look,
sagebrush scratches like etchings
gilded with dust and wasp wings,
blisters rising like the swollen stars of a clear sky,
feet so beautiful because they came.

That Your Love May Abound

Phil 1:9

The woman down the street

It's hard to love the rusted camper shell,
petunias wilting in old kitchen sinks.

So I go in your skin, woman smoking on the front stoop
with a matted dog roped to the tree.

I wear your calluses that snag the drapes
and scrape your children's hands you hold

when your husband rips the door off the hinges.
I wear the burned-out leather beneath your eyes

aching from staring at foreclosure papers
and feel the relief of dozing off

in the afternoon wrapped in the fleece of whiskey.
When I see the stalagmites of bottles

in your recycling bin, I run my fingers
over the scars on your arms—

rough but stippled with rose and light
like sunrise in the Badlands.

Artemis of Ephesus

Acts 19:23 –29

Jesus would have just smiled
at the cluster of breasts
cascading down her torso
like grapes: *It is true*

you have not two, but forty.
Return to the meteor
from which you were carved
and fertilize no more.

And she would start over
as a space rock fallen
from the sky—untouched—
and all her silver cousins

rescued from those sweaty
pilgrim hands he would melt
back to the ground where they lived
before slaves shimmied

down shafts to separate
the lead from the luster
veining the earth, running
in the stones like his blood.

Areopagus Acts 17:22 –29

There is no waking without him.
The creases in your sheets remind you
his job is to mess with your life. He stalks you
into the kitchen where the coffee splashes your hand
then flings you to the cold baptism of the faucet.
No, you will not forget him when he swerves you to the edge
of the snow bank and overrides your heartbeat,
when he hunts you down with *morning by morning*
new mercies I see, the rhythm cutting
your thoughts like a blender's metallic pulse.
You wish he never knew that sometimes
you want to grip a god you can leave behind,
the cool bronze calves of a statue
you can visit in a temple down the street,
a straight-faced fellow happy with an offering
of a charred bird or two. You could finally be alone
with your luxurious fears, escape into the woods
without his breath blowing the leaves into your path,
the expectant open fields of his hands
waiting for you to sweep in your crumbs.

Visiting the Museum After a Charismatic Church Service

Ferment, Roxy Paine
Nelson-Atkins Museum of Art

Spirit,
   you do not strike
down the center of my body
   and convulse me
into praise.
   You hook me
like a dendrite branch,
   slowly, craggily wrapping
around my bones.
   I cannot reach
without meeting
   the stainless steel loop of you
between my fingers,
   your tongue of fire split
into a thousand silver
   hairs.

The Fruit of the Spirit

Gal 5:22

If the Spirit left me a bushel of pears
on the counter, I'd find it easier to believe
than any possession of peace

or self-control—waking without belly
dread or keeping Cherry Garcia
in the freezer for more than twelve hours.

And joy and gentleness? When my son
spills a lime green Megaslush in the car,
I should sing, *Let's call the paper towel fairy!*

but instead bang the dash: *Crap!*
Pay more attention! and tail the fluff-headed
Bonneville driver all the way home.

The fruit aren't commands, but signs,
I've been taught, evidence of genuine faith.
I thought I'd crucified this nonsense

with the flesh. Have you forsaken me,
Christ? Or have I never believed?
Come on, you didn't say shit, He says.

And the ice cream made it past
the ten-hour mark. That's as sweet
as peaches in August, my friend,

that's juice running down my beard.

Temple of the Holy Spirit

1 Cor 6:19

Thyroidectomy, Highland Park Hospital

My spirit was subdued with beams
of anesthesia, held aloft in the heaven
reserved for comas and graves awaiting rapture.

They carved out the gland that transforms
my daily bread to power and peace—the spirit,
really—a red butterfly with one bulging wing.

Was it still a part of me when they placed it
in the dish? Was there still a desperate
throbbing toward God in those prodigal cells

like the hearts of all the infamous redeemed?
David with one hand below and one toward heaven
as he watched the water run down Bathsheba's neck,

Noah slurring *glory, glory Elohim* in his drunken tent—
sin sticking to us like these swelling nodules
as our bodies sway with wayward praise.

Pilgrimage

National Shrine to St. Paul, St. Paul, MN

I. Shipwreck of Faith   *1 Tim 1:19*

Hopelessly low church, borne of a congregation
where ushers tear up Hawaiian rolls
moments before communion, I slump into the pew
in those echoing hours between masses
with no genuflection, no cross.
Shoes clacking marble, and stained-glass saints
touching the bony tips of their fingers,
send me to the cold, far fields of the spirit
where staring at the spaces between reeds
is the closest thing to prayer. I shiver in this ribcage
of a dome. My 4G works, but dammit—He'll see me
refresh. In the chapel of the Sacred Heart,
another woman kneels and rocks, pulsing as if tethered
to his aorta, channeling His blood.

II. Signs and Wonders   *2 Cor 12:12*

I came here to get to know the guy
who fought off wild animals for Jesus,

who roasted on the open sea
while drifting on the wreckage,

singing. I wanted to know something
of lurching snakes and hurled stones,

of beatings and hunger and sleepless,
delirious prayer. Not just another

professional prophet with a stone robe
and outstretched arm elevated

so high on his block, I have to step back
and bang into a pillar to face him—

III. The Spirit Searches Everything   *1 Cor 2:10*

The only thing I get
is the Holy Spirit painted
on the ceiling above the altar,

a primitive black bird
in the center of the sun,
muscle with outstretched wings.

Fan out your feathers,
lonely crow, descend and gouge,
needle down to my marrow.

I need to keep you near me
so if I have to
I can squeeze you in my fist.

IV. Carry the Death of Christ   *2 Cor 4:10*

Get him off the cross and out of the grave,
my church would say. It's not about his death.
Stop your moping, Pieta Mary,
and put your son down, his head flopping back
like a newborn's. You're always touching
his faultlines of scars, thinking not about heaven
but the weight in your arms and the blood
on your clothes, the memory of his birth (still?)
beating fast against your chest.

V. Regeneration   *Titus 3:5*

Five minutes before I have to leave,
so I sidle over and clunk

the kneeler down
before the Sacred Heart.

Once a girl died of ecstasy
during her first communion,
His heart-shrapnel exploding
in her chest. I can barely speak

to him without thinking
of the leotard I haven't washed

for my daughter's ballet class.
I tossed it in the bathroom sink

before driving the 480 miles
to St. Paul, and there it still

lies in its embarrassment
of pizza sauce. My daughter

was dancing with her food,
I tell him. I wanted to watch her

spin, her copper hair fanning out
with each rotation

as she took the bites between.
It's all I can see now

as my husband idles the van
outside, you, Sunburst Beating

Fist of Love, Holy Notification
flashing on my dim wall,

Tour Guide of all
my stupefied pilgrimages

as I ramble past the stone angels
and close the car door on my foot,

forever and ever, amen.

Sacrifice of Praise

Rom 12:1

Katydids crunch out their songs
in the maple tops.
Crickets chirrup and trill,
and something I can't identify
casts a glow over it all
like a ringing Tibetan bowl.

I lie downstairs all night
with the windows open,
legs and wings drawing down
my tangled nerves like combs.

Tomorrow I will wake with no mind
for scripture, no fire for prayer:
hungover from a night of praise,
body thrumming in the August haze.

Onesimus Speaks

Since I stole your money, Philemon, and even more, myself, the body
that broke earth and stacked stones at daybreak while you slept,

you have every right to lash me till the whites of my intestines show,
brand FUG on my forehead, or throw me to the lions, who love
especially

the taste of escaped slaves, our blood sweet with freedom's fleeting
breath.
But Paul, wild-eyed with Christ, has washed down his prison walls

with prayer. He knows you will take me back, not a slave, but a brother
delivering *koinonia* to your congregation in *this present evil age,*
teaching

how to pray paralytics into motion and how to sleep in peace
when soldiers sharpen swords outside your windows. Paul calls me his
son, no—

his very heart. I am no longer your body but will reside in yours,
pump forgiveness and prayer through your veins. I will make you

see Christ in every jangling harlot and rotting, leprous face.
I will make you a slave to God's bidding.

May the Word Run Swiftly

2 Thess 3:1

Like the invisible coyotes that streak through the woods
to the fringes of our town, a bawling wind of voices.
They've come too close, the village complains.
Perhaps. I've heard the squeals of chipmunks
caught in the fur-fire. People plug their ears,
follow their dogs out at night. But still, I open
my window to their shrill, persistent haunting,
fall asleep to the blessed assurance
of a pulsing, moon-ticked pack
loping over the fallen leaves in the darkness,
working together for some kind of good.

Before All Things

The day Christ died a record-long freight train
barreled through the Rollins Road crossing.
For seven minutes tankers and lumber flats
vibrated through the spikes in his wrists.

A fisherman dropped his pole by the retention pond
and headed toward the hill. A girl at a bus stop
clutched her side as the embryo implanted himself.
We'll be late for the movie, I said.

That night, a meteor lit a tongue of fire
over the Midwestern sky. Our kitchen flashed,
and you froze at the sink. *Christ was just born,*
you said. I ground my best coffee as an offering

and kept watch through the night. Legion roared
through the maple leaves; the Pharisees' stones
thudded to the ground. The loaves in the kitchen
ruptured their bags, then the Earth burst into being.

Width, Length, Height, Depth

Eph 3:18

Jenny's Canyon, Snow Canyon State Park, Utah

There is something small
about the love of God.

I clamber up a few rocks,
walk a hundred yards

through pink sand,
then feel the canyon walls

converge on my shoulders.
Just skin, hawk song,

my blood pounding
against fossils in the dark,

my only movements my hands
channeling the marrow

of sandstone. I can look nowhere
but up the sheer red walls

pocked and hallowed
by chronicles of rain,

forever closing
but never touching,

in the gap
the whole sky caught.

Scripture Reference Index

All scripture is English Standard Version (ESV) unless otherwise noted.

Scripture Reference Index